FATAL FAULTS

The Story of the *Challenger* Explosion

BY ERIC BRAUN

Consultant:
Jim Gerard
NASA Aerospace Education
Specialist, Retired

CAPSTONE PRESS
a capstone imprint

Tangled History is published by Capstone Press,
1710 Roe Crest Drive, North Mankato, Minnesota 56003
www.capstonepub.com

Library of Congress Cataloging-in-Publication Data
Braun, Eric, 1971–
Fatal faults : the story of the *Challenger* explosion / by Eric Braun.
pages cm. — (Tangled history)
Includes bibliographical references and index.
Summary: "In a narrative nonfiction format, follows people who experienced the
Challenger tragedy and controversy"— Provided by publisher.
ISBN 978-1-4914-7077-0 (library binding) — ISBN 978-1-4914-7081-7 (pbk.) —
ISBN 978-1-4914-7085-5 (ebook pdf)
1. Challenger (Spacecraft)—Accidents—Juvenile literature. 2. Space shuttles—
Accidents—Investigation—Juvenile literature. 3. United States. National Aeronautics
and Space Administration—Officials and employees—Juvenile literature.
4. Engineers—Professional ethics—United States—Juvenile literature.
5. Whistle blowing—United States—Case studies—Juvenile literature.
6. Honesty—Juvenile literature. I. Title. II. Title: Story of the *Challenger* explosion.
TL867.B73 2016
363.12'4—dc23   2014041433

Editorial Credits
Jennifer Besel, editor; Tracy Davies McCabe, designer; Tracy Cummins, media
researcher; Tori Abraham, production specialist

Photo Credits
Alamy: Everett Collection Historical, 64; AP Photo: 60, Bruce Weaver, Cover, Charles
Tasnadi, 95, Dennis Cook, 86, Jim Cole, 45, Scott Stewart, 85; Corbis: Bettmann, 54,
97; Getty Images: Space Frontiers, 6, Terry Ashe/The LIFE Images Collection, 72, 80;
NASA: 1, 4, 16, 22, 28, 38, 53, 98; Shutterstock: Feng Yu, Design Element, Picsfive,
Back Cover; Wikimedia: NASA, 103.

Print in Canada.
032015   008825FRF15

TABLE OF CONTENTS

PRESSURE

Managers and engineers at NASA had seen the warning signs on previous shuttle launches—burn marks where sections of the solid rocket boosters (SRBs) joined together. Pressure had caused rocket fuel to leak through parts of the joints. They knew the leaking might happen again. They knew it could cause a massive catastrophe. And they knew the cold weather that day could increase the risk.

But so far, through 24 previous space shuttle missions, the burns had done no real harm. Nothing had actually gone wrong.

NASA felt intense pressure to keep flying. Throughout the early 1980s, the space shuttle program had been struggling. It was taking longer than expected to prepare shuttles to fly again after they returned. Various problems with the shuttles caused delays, increased costs, and spawned concerns over safety. NASA was embarrassed. And it was worried. If the government lost confidence in the space shuttle program, it would stop paying for it. NASA needed to show that it could keep up the schedule.

When it came to the *Challenger* launch, there was another source of pressure. One of the astronauts was Christa McAuliffe, who was to be the first Teacher in Space. As the first civilian to fly into space, McAuliffe was an important symbol. She showed that the space shuttle could allow ordinary people access to outer space. That was exactly what NASA wanted people to think about the shuttle program—not delayed launches and wasted money.

Only things weren't going as planned. The weather had been much colder than it usually is in Florida. There was ice on the launchpad. By January 28, 1986, *Challenger*'s launch had been delayed four times, and engineers pleaded for it to be delayed again.

Instead, *Challenger* lifted off into the cold, blue sky.

DECISION TO LAUNCH

The space shuttle *Challenger*, with its two white solid rocket boosters near the wings, traveled through early morning fog on its way to the icy launchpad for its 10th launch.

Allan McDonald

The more time passed, the more
Allan McDonald worried.

His bosses at Morton Thiokol—the
company that made the space shuttles'
solid rocket boosters—had requested
a five-minute break from the group
phone call they were having. They
wanted to have a private discussion.
But now it had been nearly 30 minutes,
and still Thiokol was off-line.

The question they were discussing
was complicated because there were
many factors to consider. And yet it
was very simple. Should *Challenger*
launch tomorrow?

The answer, McDonald knew, was "No." It shouldn't. The Thiokol engineers had just spent two hours on the phone explaining the dangers. They believed it was too risky to launch when the temperature was going to be so cold. So why did the Thiokol managers want to talk in private? And what was taking so long?

The three-way conference call involved the Thiokol people in Utah, NASA people at the Marshall Space Flight Center (MSFC) in Alabama, and NASA people at Kennedy Space Center (KSC) in Florida. McDonald worked for Thiokol, but he was at KSC with the NASA managers. Outside the meeting room there, *Challenger* sat on its launchpad, nose pointed into the sky, glowing in the white light of high-powered lamps. Each of the two massive solid rocket boosters attached to the bottom were filled with 500 tons of solid fuel. Between those sat an even bigger vessel, the external fuel tank for the shuttle's main engines, which would be filled with 143,000 gallons of liquid oxygen and 383,000 gallons of liquid hydrogen.

As the director of the SRB project at Thiokol, it was McDonald's job to represent his company at KSC and give a "yes" or "no" to the shuttle's launch. For this launch, when it would get as cold as 18 degrees, McDonald knew there might be a problem with the SRBs. That's why he arranged the conference call with Thiokol. He wanted to hear what the engineers thought. They were the experts. They knew more about the SRBs than anyone else. McDonald planned to do whatever the engineers recommended.

According to the engineers, the danger had to do with the O-rings—rubber rings that helped seal the sections of the SRBs together. After previous shuttle flights, they had found evidence of blowby—soot outside the primary O-rings. This meant that the O-rings had not made a perfect seal, and some rocket fuel had blown through, leaving burns. Luckily, the secondary O-rings had always held and nothing terrible had happened. But if a leak was bad enough, an explosion could occur.

The worst blowby came on a launch one year earlier, when the temperature was 53 degrees—the coldest shuttle launch ever. Thiokol engineers had evidence that the O-rings tended to get stiff in cold temperatures and not hold their seals as well. Over the course of the two-hour phone call, they had described this evidence. They had faxed over charts and photos showing burn marks.

Thiokol engineer Roger Boisjoly described most of the evidence. He had a reputation for being a whip-smart problem solver.

"The colder temperatures predicted can change the O-ring material from something like a hard sponge to something like a brick," Boisjoly said on the phone.

But NASA pushed back. Lawrence Mulloy, the SRB project manager for NASA, asked Boisjoly and his colleagues if they knew the cold weather affected the seals. He said the evidence showed that blowby had occurred on launches of different temperatures, including warm-weather launches.

The engineers admitted that was true.

"How then can you conclude that temperature has anything to do with blowby?" asked Mulloy.

Boisjoly didn't back down. He said the blowby was worse when the weather was colder. McDonald, sitting at the table with Mulloy, noticed that this answer seemed to make Mulloy angry.

Mulloy then asked Joe Kilminster, one of the Thiokol vice presidents on the call, "What's your recommendation?"

"We recommend no-go," Kilminster said.

"My God," Mulloy shouted. "When do you want me to launch, next April?"

McDonald saw determination burning in Mulloy's eyes. He realized that NASA wanted to launch tomorrow no matter what. He couldn't believe it.

Even without seeing Mulloy in person, Kilminster also understood his determination to launch. That's when he asked for the five-minute break.

"Maybe they're going to try to find more evidence to support the no-go," thought McDonald.

But the longer the break lasted, the more he worried they were going to give in.

In Utah the private discussion among Morton
Thiokol employees had taken a new turn.

"We need to make a management decision,"
said Jerry Mason, the highest-ranking vice
president in the room.

Roger Boisjoly knew what that meant.
The engineers' opinion would be downplayed.
Managers had to think about keeping their
customer—NASA—happy. NASA had been
paying Thiokol millions of dollars to build the
SRBs. But in the previous few months, it had
talked about using another company instead. If
NASA was unhappy with the job Thiokol was
doing, it might start buying its rocket boosters
from another provider.

And NASA was clearly unhappy with
the recommendation not to launch. Boisjoly
sensed the managers were ready to change their

recommendation. He laid a set of photos on the table, pointing to the sooty marks where the O-rings had failed.

"Look carefully at these photographs!" he said to his bosses. "Don't ignore what they are telling us!"

The managers didn't say anything. The previous July Boisjoly had written a memo for management on the O-ring issue. In it, he wrote that if the O-ring problem was not solved, "The result would be a catastrophe of the highest order—loss of human life." He went on to write, "It is my honest and very real fear that if we do not take immediate action to dedicate a team to solve the problem with the field joint ... then we stand in jeopardy of losing a flight along with all the launchpad facilities."

But his memo from July had been essentially ignored, just as he was being ignored now. Upset and deflated, Boisjoly sat down.

"Am I the only one who wants to fly?" Mason asked the group.

The other managers in the room felt intimidated by this statement. Boisjoly watched as the managers changed their votes, one by one, from "no" to "yes."

There was nothing he could do.

Finally, the Thiokol group got back on the phone.

"We've reassessed the data," Joe Kilminster said. "We've concluded that, even though the lower temperatures are a concern, the temperature effects are inconclusive. Therefore, MTI recommends launching."

Allan McDonald felt his heart sink into his stomach.

Someone from MSFC in Alabama spoke up. "We'll need you to put that recommendation in writing, Joe, and fax it to Florida and Alabama. And we'll need it to be signed."

Hearing that, McDonald's heart sank even lower. NASA had never asked for a signed recommendation to launch before. Normally, a verbal "yes" was all that was needed. McDonald assumed they wanted a written recommendation this time because they were worried about the risk too. If anything went wrong, they could point to the sheet of paper and say, "Morton Thiokol recommended we launch. They said it was safe."

McDonald also assumed that he would be the one asked to sign the recommendation. He and Lawrence Mulloy looked at each other across the table.

"I won't sign that recommendation, Larry," McDonald said. "It will have to come from the plant in Utah."

While they waited for the recommendation to be faxed over, McDonald continued to make his case to Mulloy and the other NASA employees in the room. In addition to the concern over the O-rings, there was ice all over the launchpad. And the oceans were extremely rough, meaning that the ships at sea would have a difficult time recovering the SRBs after they were released from the shuttle.

But his arguments got nowhere. Finally he said, "If anything happens to this launch, I wouldn't want to be the person that has to stand in front of a board of inquiry to explain why we launched this."

After 30 minutes the recommendation spooled out of the fax machine. It was already signed by Joe Kilminster.

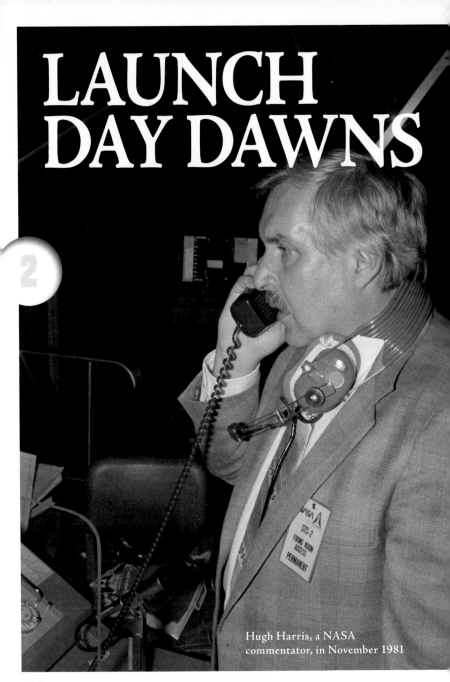

LAUNCH DAY DAWNS

Hugh Harris, a NASA
commentator, in November 1981

Hugh Harris

As Hugh Harris drove to work at KSC, the temperature outside was in the low 30s and dropping. He didn't know about the meeting that had happened the night before between NASA and Morton Thiokol. All he knew was that it was cold—very cold. Colder than anyone could remember it being here.

Harris was known as "the voice of NASA." It was his job to describe countdowns and launches. When shuttle launches took place, Harris' voice was heard by millions of people all over the world.

Driving through Florida before dawn, he noticed that many of the orange groves were blanketed in smoke from bonfires burning to protect the fruit from freezing. Water in the ditches alongside the road was frozen.

Harris didn't think NASA would launch on such a cold day. He didn't know about the O-ring issue, but he knew that ice could be a problem. When the shuttle blasted off, chunks of ice could go flying and damage the shuttle's protective tiles.

So when he arrived at the press site at KSC, he asked an information specialist named Andrea Shea King if she had heard any news.

"Have they announced a scrub yet?"

She said that so far, the launch had not been canceled. "Everything has been going smoothly," she said. "But there's a little concern about ice on the launchpad. Can you see the icicles?"

Harris looked at the screens that showed various views of the shuttle and launchpad. *Challenger* still stood on its end with its SRBs and external fuel tank. Alongside the shuttle was the fixed service structure, a tall tower with a high-speed elevator that took astronauts up 197 feet to the walkway that led to the crew cabin. Troughs filled with water sat beneath the solid rocket motors. During launch that water would be sprayed across the launchpad. It would help absorb the powerful sound energy that exploded from *Challenger*'s engines so it wasn't reflected back to the shuttle, damaging the tail and those protective tiles.

But now water was a problem. Though it had been mixed with antifreeze to keep it from freezing, icicles hung from the horizontal beams. An ice team was out there, breaking off icicles from the tower and the launchpad. Others were breaking up the ice in the troughs with 50-foot poles. Though he was warm inside the pressroom, Harris shivered.

Harris checked another screen. There he saw the astronauts eating their traditional launch-morning breakfast of steak and eggs. Today's astronauts were Commander Francis Scobee, a shuttle veteran who everyone called Dick; Pilot Mike Smith; Mission Specialists Judith Resnik, Ellison Onizuka, and Ronald McNair; and Payload Specialists Gregory Jarvis and Christa McAuliffe—the teacher.

Christa McAuliffe

Christa McAuliffe sat at the table, her steak and eggs breakfast in front of her. She had learned so much in the past few months, but she could scarcely believe that she was going to space today … if nothing else went wrong.

A year and a half ago, she never dreamed she could go into space. But then President Ronald Reagan announced the Teacher in Space program, designed to increase people's interest in education. NASA and the U.S. government also wanted to increase interest in the space program and open the door for space flight to ordinary people.

McAuliffe, a high school social studies teacher from New Hampshire, was one of about 11,000 teachers to apply to be the first Teacher in Space. In July 1985 she was chosen as the winner. According to NASA officials, they chose her not only because she was a great teacher, but also because she had an enthusiastic personality. "If you're offered a seat on a rocket ship," she said once, "don't ask what seat. Just get on."

But McAuliffe was quiet that day as she reflected on the people who would rocket into space with her. There was Greg Jarvis, who would conduct experiments on how weightlessness affected liquids. Dick Scobee and Michael Smith were both former Air Force pilots. Smith had logged 4,300 hours of flying time before coming to NASA. Scobee had more than 6,500! Ronald McNair and Ellison Onizuka, like Scobee, had been on shuttle missions before. Together the three had spent a combined 433 hours in space. Like her, McNair and Onizuka both had young children, so they had that in common.

McAuliffe had a special admiration for Judy Resnik, the only other woman on the team. Resnik held a doctorate in electrical engineering. McAuliffe was blown away by how she could figure out what all the circuits did on the shuttle. She was also confident that Resnik would keep all those circuits working as they should.

THE CREW BOARDS

Challenger crew from front to back: Dick Scobee, Judith Resnik, Ronald McNair, Mike Smith, Christa McAuliffe, Ellison Onizuka, Gregory Jarvis

Christa McAuliffe

Challenger Launch Platform,
January 28, 8:03 a.m.

The high-speed elevator reached the top of the tower. The astronauts entered the White Room, the area where they prepared to board the space shuttle. Christa McAuliffe was nervous. She had faith in her training, and she certainly trusted the veteran astronauts she was flying with. But still … she was nervous. After all, she was blasting into space!

McAuliffe planned to teach two 15-minute lessons while in orbit. The lessons would be broadcast on TV to students all over. Part of the lessons would be a tour of the spacecraft, which she called "The Ultimate Field Trip." She was well prepared, well trained, and, yes, excited.

But the typically chipper teacher was quieter than usual that morning. It was hard to avoid the enormity of what she was about to do.

The launch cancellations of the past couple days added to her nervousness. Yesterday, McAuliffe and the others lain on their backs in the shuttle for five hours waiting for NASA technicians to fix a broken hatch handle. Eventually the launch was pushed to today. The press made a big deal out of that one. Any handyman should have been able to fix a broken door handle. But for NASA, it cost millions of dollars to fix and kept the world's greatest space vehicle grounded. Even Peter Jennings, a network anchorman, opened his show by saying, "Once again a flawless liftoff proved to be too much of a challenge for *Challenger*."

Today they had ice to worry about.

"Watch the ice," said one of the technicians on hand to help the crew board. Part of the arm that led to the shuttle was icy and slippery.

"This is a beautiful day to fly!" Captain Scobee said, smiling. Then he produced a small gift wrapped in a red bow and handed it to the technician. "Here," he said, "you guys might need this." It was an alloy bolt for the hatch door. Everyone laughed at the joke about yesterday's mishap.

An engineer named Manley Carter climbed into the cabin with Captain Scobee and pilot Mike Smith to help them get situated.

"Boy! The sun feels good this morning," Smith said.

"You should have been here at 2 a.m.," Carter replied.

McAuliffe shivered and danced from foot to foot to keep warm while Carter helped Ellison Onizuka on board next. Then it was Judith Resnik, who sat up near the pilots.

Before climbing in, Resnik turned to McAuliffe, who would be sitting in back. "Next time I see you, we'll be in space," she said.

"Good morning, Judy," said Carter.

"Cowabunga!" replied Resnik.

Finally, it was McAuliffe's turn. Climbing aboard, just doing something, anything, provided a little relief from the tension she felt while waiting. Then one of the technicians handed her a big red delicious apple—the traditional gift for teachers. McAuliffe broke into a broad smile.

"Save it for me," she said. "I'll eat it when I get back."

Among her personal items, McAuliffe was carrying her husband's class ring, her daughter's necklace, and her son's stuffed frog, Fleegle. Days earlier she had taken out a million-dollar life insurance policy. If anything happened to her, her family would be taken care of.

Carter carefully walked her through all the steps as he helped her into her seat. By 8:36 the entire crew was on board and Carter closed the hatch. The handle worked fine.

Hugh Harris

Hugh Harris looked again at the screen showing crews breaking up icicles hanging from the platform. Crew members dragged a long shrimp net through the troughs of water, pulling out thick hunks of ice. The launch time had been pushed back by two hours, but it wasn't getting much warmer. There was still an hour until launch. There was still time to scrub.

BLAST OFF

4

Challenger lifted off from the Kennedy Space Center at 11:38 a.m. on January 28, 1986.

Grace Corrigan

In an office in Kennedy Space Center, the families of the astronauts were also waiting. Perhaps because of the unusual cold and the earlier scrubs, they all seemed extra nervous. A few talked quietly, but mostly they paced in silence and glanced up at the big screens that showed the shuttle sitting on the launchpad. They could clearly see the ice on the shuttle and launchpad.

Dick Scobee's son, Richard, a senior in the Air Force Academy, leaned with his back to a wall, deep in thought. Ronald McNair's wife pushed their youngest child in a stroller, while their son stood nearby. McAuliffe's husband, Steve, carried their daughter, Caroline. Their son, Scott, rubbed his sleepy eyes.

Finally, as the launch drew near, the families moved outside to the observation deck. They walked together into the biting cold, exchanging excited smiles and nervous glances. Outside, they stamped their feet and wrapped their arms around themselves.

McAuliffe's mother, Grace Corrigan, stood with her husband in a separate area from the other family members with Scott's third-grade class. The press was on the deck too. Their cameras and video cameras recorded the Corrigans' expressions. Ed and Grace wore sweaters and coats. Their breath puffed out in white clouds.

Like the rest of the family members, Grace Corrigan felt uneasy due to all the cancellations and cold weather. Things weren't going the way she imagined they would. Something just didn't seem right. She looked out over the field at *Challenger* sitting 3 miles away and imagined her daughter sitting inside, strapped into her seat.

"I'd take her off that thing if I could get out there," Ed said.

"Even if you could, she wouldn't come,"
Grace replied.

It was T-minus five minutes. Five minutes until liftoff. A moment ago the big walkway the astronauts used to walk from the elevator and enter *Challenger* had swung away from the orbiter. Now pilot Mike Smith switched on the auxiliary power units, or APUs.

"APUs are coming on," he said.

Smith's excitement was building. Even though he was an experienced pilot, this was his first time going into space. All the waiting seemed to be over. No more scrubs. They were going to launch.

From the control tower he heard, "*Challenger*, this is Control. You are on internal power, over. Roger, out."

Smith scanned the instrument panel as lights registered the switch. *Challenger* began to hum with hydraulic power as various panels and flaps went through a series of automated moves to make sure they were ready to steer the ship.

"We've got three good APUs," Smith said.

"Visors are coming down," Commander Scobee said. This was an instruction to the astronauts to close their visors and seal their helmets.

At T-minus two minutes, Scobee said to the crew, "Welcome to space, guys."

At T-minus one minute and 28 seconds, he reminded his crew to make sure the harnesses were locked. Then he joked, "I won't lock mine; I might have to reach something."

"Ooh-kaaaaay," said Smith.

Smith watched his panel as the instruments measured fuel pressure and verified that everything was operational. Everything looked perfect.

T-minus eight seconds: The enormous tank of water was dumped over the launchpad to absorb sound waves so they wouldn't rip apart the craft. Chunks of ice still floated in it.

T-minus six seconds: Smith felt the orbiter vibrate and heard a powerful rumble as *Challenger*'s three main engines ignited. The rumble intensified into a roar as the engines reached full power.

"There they go, guys," Scobee said.

The vibration and noise grew with the power of more than 2 million pounds of thrust as the orbiter strained and flexed upward. But it didn't leave the ground yet. Explosive restraining bolts attached to the SRBs held it fast to the launchpad. Though a scrub at this point was very rare, it was still possible to call off the launch if the computers sensed anything wrong. *But the computers didn't sense any trouble.*

T-minus five seconds. Four. Three. Two. One.

Allan McDonald had sat through many launches in his career. The moment when the SRBs ignite always made him nervous. As the manager of the SRBs at Morton Thiokol, he was acutely aware of the power of all that rocket fuel—and all that could go wrong. Any small mistake could cause a catastrophe.

But this time, as he sat at his console in the Control Center, he was more than nervous. He was afraid. He'd been watching his screen all morning, switching camera views to see the crews fishing hunks of ice from the sound suppression troughs and chipping ice from the launchpad. The crew even removed ice from the orbiter, the external fuel tank, and the SRBs.

He had been there when Charlie Stevenson, the head of the ice team, told a NASA director, "The only choice you got today is not to go!" But Stevenson's thoughts hadn't changed anything.

He kept thinking about the O-rings, how they got stiff when the temperature was cold. He kept remembering the photos that Roger Boisjoly had shown everyone—the soot marks from blowby when the O-rings failed.

As the countdown reached the final seconds, and the shuttle's main engines ignited, McDonald began to sweat. He kept an eye on the video screen that showed the shuttle, but he more carefully tracked the SRB fuel pressure data on his console screen. The SRBs would produce more than 3 million pounds of thrust each. If either of them experienced abnormal pressure—by even a hair—the result would be an explosion. If any of the O-rings were going to fail, he would know before anyone else because he'd see the pressure drop on his console. Of course it wouldn't matter then because the whole thing would blow up.

As the final seconds of the countdown ticked by, McDonald held his breath. On-screen he saw the orbiter tilt about 3 feet to the side as the main engines struggled against the restraining bolts. Then the SRBs ignited.

Mike Smith braced himself as the firing SRBs raised the roar inside the orbiter to a terrifying level. *Challenger*'s computers sent the signal to explode the restraining bolts, setting the craft free. The booster rockets were five times more powerful than the orbiter's main engines, adding up to a total of 44 million horsepower. The ship burned 11,000 pounds of fuel per second as it lifted off the ground.

The force of liftoff pushed Smith and the other astronauts hard against their seats. The ship shook and thundered. Sitting on these massive engines—the most powerful engines the world had ever seen—was an incredible feeling.

"All right!" yelled Resnik.

"Here we go!" said Smith.

Allan McDonald

A great cloud of white smoke billowed out from the SRBs as the shuttle straightened out and lifted off the ground. At first it seemed to hover, just for a second, on the fluffy cloud, but then it took off.

Challenger cleared the tower. Allan McDonald let his breath out. He was sure that if the O-rings were going to fail, it would be right at liftoff. As he watched the shuttle climb higher and higher, gaining more and more speed, he relaxed.

What he didn't see—and what his console didn't show—was that a series of small puffs of black smoke had escaped from one of the joints on the right SRB. The O-rings there had grown too stiff to hold the seal with the flexing rocket parts, and a small amount of fuel had blown through. Two and a half seconds after liftoff, chemical residue from the burn clogged the joint, essentially resealing it, and the pressure was contained again. But the joint was damaged and wouldn't hold for long.

I CAN'T SEE THE SHUTTLE!

5

the scene above the Kennedy Space Center moments after *Challenger's* liftoff

Mike Smith

Challenger had reached 10,000 feet and half the speed of sound. Mike Smith monitored their progress. A few seconds later, he let the crew know they'd passed the speed of sound. "There's Mach one."

The shuttle rolled onto its back as it climbed ever higher. As it reached 19,000 feet, it approached a turbulent layer of atmosphere called a wind shear. It wasn't safe to cross the wind shear with too much speed. If they did *Challenger* could break apart.

"Throttle down to ninety-four," said a flight dynamics officer in Houston. The shuttle reduced power to 94 percent of its maximum.

Smith and the other astronauts felt the ship convulse like a massive roller coaster.

"Looks like we've got a lot of wind here today," Smith shouted over the noise. In fact, it was the most violent wind shear ever breached by a space shuttle.

By now they had slowed to 65 percent of maximum power. They passed through the turbulence, and everything was going exactly to plan.

"Throttle up," came the command from Houston. Time to go hard again. Smith studied his computer screens, which showed their speed, course, and other information.

Once again, he could not contain his excitement. "Woo-hoo!" he hollered.

"Roger," Commander Scobee said to Houston. "Go at throttle up."

The orbiter's flaps and tiles helped guide it through the turbulence, but—though nobody knew it—the wind further stressed the damaged joint of the right SRB. The chemical residue that had temporarily resealed the joint gave way. A small plume of flame spurted past the secondary O-ring to the outside of the SRB. Nobody on the ground or in the orbiter noticed.

Within two seconds flames grew and spit back in the slipstream toward the external fuel tank. Three seconds later it burned through the tank's insulation. Then it burned through the tank itself.

No one knows what Smith saw or felt next. But the last words transmitted from *Challenger* were his. *"Uh-oh."*

Grace Corrigan

At liftoff Grace Corrigan cheered ecstatically along with everyone else on the deck. For a brief moment, the cold seemed to lift off too. Though humans had been flying into space for decades, it was still a great thrill to witness. Powerful sound waves from the craft shook the roof they stood on. The shuttle looked majestic rising higher and higher into the sky, streaking atop a massive trail of white smoke and carrying on board an ordinary person just like them—Corrigan's daughter.

Suddenly, without understanding why, Corrigan began to sob. Her husband held her tightly, and her daughter Lisa squeezed her hand.

Allan McDonald

Allan McDonald, who was still closely monitoring flight data on his console, noticed that the chamber pressure on the right-hand SRB was almost 3 percent lower than that on the left.

Before he could process what that meant, he and others who were watching the shuttle on-screen noticed that flames on the right SRB seemed to be spreading upward along the rocket. Though he'd never seen a shuttle explode, a feeling of horrible recognition opened up inside his stomach.

Grace Corrigan

Just a minute after the shuttle rose into the sky, the families and visitors on the observation deck saw something that confused them. *Challenger* seemed to flicker with light then disappear for a moment. As they strained their eyes to the sky, the shuttle ignited into a ball of fire. White smoke billowed from the still-climbing craft.

Some people on the observation deck were still smiling and giving thumbs up. As they gradually realized what was happening, their smiles froze, then turned to open-mouthed grimaces. Their arms dropped, and their hearts seemed to stop. The press turned their cameras once more to the Corrigans as their faces darkened with horror.

"I can't see the shuttle!" Grace Corrigan cried.

The overwhelming roar of the craft had stopped, leaving instead a roaring quiet. The cries of pride and awe from seconds earlier now turned to wails of fear and anguish. The children of the astronauts cried for their parents. Scott McAuliffe's classmates stared at the sky in confusion, then at the adults around them. What was happening?

Moments after they saw the ball of fire, Grace Corrigan (center), her husband, Ed (right), and her daughter Betsy (left) realized what had happened.

As Allan McDonald watched on
his screen, *Challenger* became invisible
behind a giant fireball. The craft was nearly
50,000 feet in the air and moving at nearly
twice the speed of sound when it happened.

At first he thought the SRBs had dropped
from the craft too soon. They should have
burned for another two minutes before
separation. He watched his screen intently,
waiting for the orbiter to emerge from the
ball of flames.

On the observation deck, a young girl, crying and pointing at the sky, cried, "The teacher! The teacher is up there!"

A moment later a NASA official was at Grace Corrigan's side. "The craft has exploded," he said to her.

"The craft has exploded," she repeated, still not comprehending. Photographers shot photo after photo of her and Ed, who wore a picture of his smiling daughter pinned to his chest.

Allan McDonald

For a few moments, nobody spoke or moved. Like everyone else in the room, Allan McDonald continued to watch the fireball on his screen. Some in the room began to sob with anguish, while others wept in silence.

Over the communications network, a voice began repeating "RTLS! RTLS! Return To Launch Site!" But as McDonald kept staring at his monitor, he knew there was no craft left to return. The fire in the sky began to peel apart, with the two SRBs still soaring into the air, creating a fork-shaped trail of smoke. But the rest of the craft was still invisible. NASA's public announcer in Houston continued to announce flight velocity and altitude.

When pieces from the explosion, including big sections of the orbiter, began to rain out of the fire and fall to earth, the announcer said, "Obviously a major malfunction. ... We have no downlink." As if any more explanation was needed, he added, "We have a report from the flight dynamics officer that the vehicle has exploded."

The SRBs continued their ascent. Finally a NASA safety officer pushed a button, and the SRBs self-destructed.

"It's a bad day!" said a NASA director. Across the room, McDonald saw someone with his hands clasped and his head bowed, praying silently.

On Board Challenger

What looked like an explosion was technically not. Rather, the external fuel tank and the orbiter had caught fire, and then the orbiter broke apart. Its component pieces stayed mostly together. Wings spiraled out of the cloud of smoke. The crew cabin was intact and kept climbing to a height of 65,000 feet before it arced in the sky and began to descend.

Inside the cabin the crew was alive. Most or all of them were awake at least for several seconds, though recordings were destroyed in the fire and nobody knows what they said or did. A highly experienced pilot with thousands of hours of flight behind him, Mike Smith probably stayed relatively calm. He would have done everything he could to save himself and the crew. Experts believe he and Captain Scobee tried to steer the craft as it plummeted down, even without benefit of wings.

The craft's computer, which was still functioning, noticed the problem and cut off power to the engines. Judy Resnik, seated directly behind Scobee and Smith, activated their emergency air bottles.

Nearly four minutes after liftoff, the cabin struck the surface of the Atlantic Ocean at a speed greater than 200 miles per hour, crushing the structure. *No one inside survived.*

Allan McDonald

Allan McDonald looked up from his monitor for a moment. A voice on the public address system said nobody was allowed to leave the control center. The voice informed everyone that the doors to the Control Center were locked, the phones had been disconnected, and the data on the computers had been frozen. Nobody was allowed to take any documents from the room, including notes made during the launch. When the workers were allowed to leave, everyone would be checked.

At this, the spell of quiet was broken. As the room erupted in chaos, security officers impounded everything, including computers. Only minutes after *Challenger* caught fire, the investigation was underway.

Launch Control Center at Kennedy
Space Center, taken in 1981

6 SHOCK

Spectators watching the shuttle launch reacted with shock and horror when they realized what had happened.

NASA escorts led a shaken Grace and Ed Corrigan off the observation deck ahead of the rest of the crowd, most of which was still watching the sky in shock. On loudspeakers a voice announced, "The vehicle has exploded."

Corrigan felt her knees tremble as she and the other astronauts' families filed quietly into the dorms where only a few hours ago the astronauts had safely been sleeping. In McAuliffe's room Christa's sneakers lay there as if she would be back any time.

"This is not how it's supposed to be," Steve McAuliffe said.

McAuliffe's NASA nameplate was on the door. Her sister Lisa slid it out and gave it to Scott, who clung to his dad. Grace went into the dorm's common area and came back with coffee and doughnuts, but nobody wanted anything. She hugged members of the other astronauts' families. Nobody knew what to do or say, so everyone stood in silence.

"I can't be here anymore," Ed finally said. Grace agreed. NASA wanted them to wait in the dorm to be debriefed, but the Corrigans insisted on leaving.

Outside, a crowd still stood around on the grounds. When the people saw the Corrigans coming toward them, they parted to make a path. Grace and Ed walked through the quiet group to the car that would take them back to the apartment where they were staying.

When they got inside the apartment and were finally alone with family, Grace let out a deep sigh. "She was doing what she wanted to do," she said of her daughter.

Hugh Harris

Kennedy Space Center, Press Briefing Room, 4:40 p.m.

Hugh Harris' bosses had told him to keep the press at bay, but he knew they would not be held away for long. Everyone wanted to know what had happened. It was the press' job to find out.

The problem was that nobody knew. And the engineers did not want to talk to anyone until they did.

"Rumors are flying," Harris pleaded with his boss. "People are upset and angry. We need to have a press conference, or things are going to get ugly."

Finally, five hours after the explosion, Harris introduced Associate Administrator of Space Flight Jesse Moore to members of the press, who filled a 350-seat grandstand.

"It is with deep, heartfelt sorrow that I address you this afternoon," Moore said. "At 11:40 this morning, the space program experienced a national tragedy with the explosion of the space shuttle *Challenger* … I regret that I have to report that based on very preliminary searches of the ocean where the *Challenger* impacted this morning, these searches have not revealed any evidence that the crew of *Challenger* survived."

Reporters waved their hands and shouted out questions for Moore. This explanation didn't tell them anything they didn't know. Moore silenced the crowd again and apologized that he was unable to answer their questions.

He just did not have any more information, yet.

A few minutes later, Harris, the reporters, and the NASA employees in the press site gathered around a TV. President Reagan was coming on to talk about the disaster. Harris wondered if Reagan would decide that space exploration was too dangerous to continue.

"Today is a day for mourning and remembering," the president said. "Nancy and I are pained to the core by the tragedy of the shuttle *Challenger*. We know we share this pain with all of the people of our country. This is truly a national loss."

The president comforted the astronauts' families, and he called the astronauts themselves pioneers. Then he had a special message for the schoolchildren of America. "I know it is hard to understand, but sometimes painful things like this happen. It's all part of the process of exploration and discovery ... The *Challenger* crew was pulling us into the future, and we'll continue to follow them."

Thinking of the schoolchildren watching reminded Harris of Scott McAuliffe and his third-grade classmates who had been watching the launch from the observation deck. A lump swelled in his throat and tears filled his eyes.

SEARCHING

Members of the Coast Guard pulled pieces of *Challenger* out of the ocean.

Mike McAllister

Almost immediately after the accident, dozens of NASA, Coast Guard, and Navy ships searched the ocean for wreckage. Normally, picking up the SRBs from the ocean was a job reserved for two NASA ships, the *Liberty Star* and the *Freedom Star*. But with so much debris to find after the accident, NASA asked for help.

Mike McAllister worked for an Air Force contractor that worked on such projects. His ship was sailing nearby when NASA asked the ship to join the search. Battling swells more than 10 feet high, it moved through the wreckage area. Water crashed over the sides of the ship.

Like everyone on board, McAllister was an experienced diver. He had salvaged wrecks before, and he'd been a part of many searches. But this was going to be different. This was a national tragedy, and all eyes would be on him and his colleagues.

But the bad weather and the widespread area where the debris fell caused problems for the search. McAllister and other divers pulled parts of *Challenger* from the sea, dripping with water and occasionally charred from the fire. But progress was slow. The craft had broken into millions of pieces.

Americans wanted to know what happened to the shuttle, and they tracked the progress on the news. Seeing the parts of the shuttle pulled from the ocean helped them feel closure to the horrible accident. But the days wore on, and the crew cabin remained missing. That was what people wanted to see most. They wanted to know that the bodies of the seven astronauts had been returned to their families.

Every day McAllister went on dives, deep down, all the way to the ocean floor. Some days he found nothing. Some days he found pieces of the shuttle. All pieces were important. But in McAllister's mind, he was looking for the crew cabin.

Like the divers, reporters were searching too. They weren't satisfied with the information NASA was providing. They believed NASA knew more than it was saying.

Hugh Harris was doing his best to help them. He led reporters to the massive warehouse where shuttle pieces were collected. From its nose cone to giant chunks of fuselage and rounded sections of the SRBs, the pieces were displayed altogether to resemble the craft's original shape. As Harris walked reporters along the collection of pieces, he pointed out a portion of the right SRB where the burn had come through. Reporters took photos and asked questions.

"Any sign of the crew cabin?" someone asked.

After six days, more than 11 tons of material had been brought in. The entire craft weighed 2,250 tons, so there was a lot still missing. But most importantly the crew cabin and the crew were still among the lost.

"Unfortunately, no," Harris said. He understood their need to know. He wanted to know too.

INVESTIGATIONS

Photos taken during liftoff showed smoke coming from the joints in the SRBs.

Allan McDonald

Though his boss, Jerry Mason, initially told Allan McDonald to go home to Utah, McDonald resisted. He called Mason in the middle of the night.

"I have to go to Huntsville to review the flight data," he said. "Please."

He felt strong responsibility for the *Challenger* accident, and he wanted to be a part of figuring out what had happened. Mason wanted McDonald to help the SRB program back home, but he must have understood the urgency in McDonald's voice.

"All right," he finally said. "But only take two days. We need you back home."

Grateful, McDonald took the first available flight to Huntsville.

Sitting on the airplane, he thought about what might have happened. At first he feared that the O-rings had caused the fire—just as the engineers had predicted. But then he dismissed that idea because he believed that the SRBs would have exploded if the O-rings failed. As everyone had seen, the SRBs kept on flying long after the orbiter broke up. By the time he arrived in Huntsville, he believed it must have been a problem with the external fuel tank or the shuttle's main engines.

At MSFC McDonald reviewed film and photos of the launch. One set of photos caught his attention. He held them up under the light, one after another. The photos showed the black smoke puffing out of the joint right at ignition and again at "throttle up." His heart sank. His worst fears had come true.

It was the O-rings after all. They were the reason for the explosion.

Within days NASA released some of these images to the press. When reporters heard that the SRBs had caused the accident, they wanted to know who made them. NASA told them—Morton Thiokol.

People began calling the plant in Utah and threatening employees. Somebody spray-painted graffiti near the plant that said, "Thiokol—Murderers." McDonald called his wife, who was home with their four children, and told her that extra police had been assigned to patrol the area where they lived. The police would protect them from anyone looking to cause trouble.

"When are you coming home, Al?" his wife asked.

More than anything, McDonald wished he could go home. He was exhausted, and he missed his family. But he had a very important job to do.

"I don't know," he said.

NASA was investigating what happened, but many people thought someone outside NASA should investigate. President Reagan decided to create a presidential commission. The commission was meant to cooperate with NASA, but it would report to Reagan. The truth would help prevent future disasters.

Richard Feynman, a Nobel Prize winner in physics, received a phone call at his home in California. It was William Graham, the head of NASA, who had been a student of Feynman's some time ago. Graham was calling to ask if Feynman would be on the commission.

Feynman was not excited about the idea. For one thing he was involved in an exciting project that involved the development of a new kind of computer. For another he was dying of cancer and didn't have long to live. He didn't want to spend many of his precious remaining days in meetings with lawyers and politicians.

"No thanks," he told Graham.

But Graham didn't give up. "We've got a mystery on our hands," he said. "And we need your experience to help us solve it."

Like most scientists Feynman loved mysteries, and eventually he agreed. Before flying to Washington, D.C., he went to NASA's Jet Propulsion Lab (JPL) to talk to engineers who had worked on the shuttle. Since JPL was run by Caltech, the university where Feynman was a professor, he had access—and an easy opportunity to learn.

The engineers showed Feynman how the SRBs worked and even described how the O-rings had failed on occasion.

"Look," one of them said, pointing to a photo. "You can see evidence of blowby here."

"So," Feynman thought, "NASA knew about the faulty O-rings, but they flew anyway." Very curious now, he pushed to learn more. He learned about the pressure inside the SRBs and all about the fuel that propelled them. He learned about the main engines too and the potential problems they had posed. Talking with the technicians and engineers, Feynman was enjoying himself thoroughly. There was nothing he enjoyed more than discussing physics with people who were experts in their field.

However, once Feynman arrived in Washington, D.C., to join the commission, things were much less enjoyable. Led by William Rogers, a former secretary of state and attorney general, the Rogers Commission was moving slowly, and very little was getting done. Feynman felt they did much more sitting around than they did investigating.

When Rogers announced that he'd arranged for the commission to tour Kennedy Space Center the following week, Feynman's frustration overflowed. He approached Rogers after the meeting.

"We're going to Florida next Thursday," he said. "That means we've got nothing to do for five days. What'll I do for five days?"

"You can do whatever you want," Rogers said.

Feynman realized that if he were going to solve any mysteries, he'd have to strike out on his own.

He called NASA chief Bill Graham. Feynman asked if he could talk to some technicians and engineers at Johnson Space Center in Houston. Instead, Graham sent NASA technicians to Washington to meet with Feynman. As Feynman and the techs discussed the joints between the sections of the SRBs, he realized that the problems with the O-rings were not new.

"They knew that the joints didn't work well," a tech told him. "And they knew it even before the very first shuttle launched."

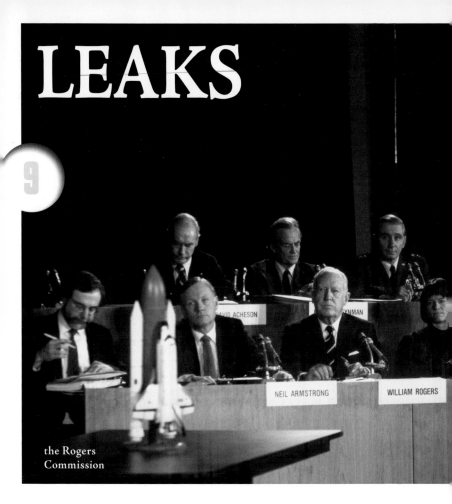

LEAKS

9

NEIL ARMSTRONG | WILLIAM ROGERS | DAVID ACHESON | YNMAN

the Rogers Commission

As the Rogers Commission reconvened on the morning of February 10, excitement and anger filled the air. There had been a huge new development in the *Challenger* story.

RIDE   ARTHUR WALKER, JR.

The previous day *The New York Times* had run a front-page story that quoted memos written by a NASA budget analyst named Richard Cook. Cook's memos, one of which was written the previous July—a full six months before the *Challenger* launch—stated that engineers at NASA were concerned that the joints on the SRBs would fail. They said that a new joint would need to be designed because the O-rings were not reliable. And they showed that everyone involved with the SRBs knew that cold weather could be a factor.

The commission discussed Cook's memo in the morning. After lunch the commission called in NASA employees to tell their sides of the story.

This group included Lawrence Mulloy, the manager who had been so upset when Thiokol advised against launching during the phone call on January 27.

William Rogers started by saying how frustrating it was to see information coming out in the newspaper before the commission knew about it. He looked at Mulloy and the other NASA employees and said, "We would hope that NASA and NASA officials will volunteer any information in a frank and forthright manner."

He made it clear that he was upset with NASA employees for not being totally honest in their testimony. He said that he didn't want NASA to feel like the commissioners were enemies. They were all on the same side, looking for the truth. But he needed NASA to be open and honest.

Because of the research he'd already done, Richard Feynman suspected that NASA was not ready to be totally honest about what had happened. He knew NASA had already covered up the O-ring problems.

Feynman was not surprised when Mulloy made a point of belittling Richard Cook.

"Cook was just a budget analyst," Mulloy said, "not an engineer." His implication was clear. Cook didn't know anything about SRBs.

He went on to say that NASA had no evidence to support that the joints on the SRBs needed to be redesigned or changed.

"Not even today?" Rogers exclaimed.

"No sir," said Mulloy. "Not even today."

"Are you suggesting that you never came to the conclusion that these things did not cause the accident?" Rogers asked in disbelief.

"Sir," said Mulloy, "I'm not aware of anything that has caused the accident yet."

Sitting toward the back of the room, Allan McDonald was stunned. How could Lawrence Mulloy say that? They all knew exactly what had happened in the disaster, and they'd all known for a long time that the SRBs needed to be redesigned. He raised his hand to speak, but nobody noticed him.

After a break commissioner Sally Ride had a question. Ride was a former astronaut and the first American woman in space. "I just had a phone call from a reporter at *The Washington Times*," she said. "This reporter heard that NASA had a discussion with one of its contractors the night before the launch. The contractor was concerned about launching in cold weather. Is that true, Mr. Mulloy?"

Mulloy admitted that there had been a discussion. He said, "After hearing the discussion, we all concluded that there was no problem with the predicted temperatures for the solid rocket motor."

Ride then asked him if he knew of any NASA memos that discussed the problems the O-rings had launching at low temperatures.

"I'm not aware of any such documents," Mulloy said.

Once again McDonald was shocked. He knew that those documents existed, and he knew Mulloy knew. It was obvious NASA was going to do everything it could to avoid responsibility—and pin it on Morton Thiokol.

He raised his hand again, but again he went unnoticed.

As Mulloy continued with his testimony, McDonald's frustration and anger grew. He raised his hand again, and then stood, waving his arms. But nobody acknowledged him. Finally McDonald walked to the front of the room to interrupt.

"I wanted to say a point about the meeting," he said, referring to the three-way phone conference the night before the launch. "The meeting was set up to send material on the fax so that people could review data and concerns and our basis for that concern."

Then McDonald drove home his main point. "The recommendation at that time from the data that was sent out from Thiokol was not to launch below 53 degrees Fahrenheit."

The commissioners looked at each other with confusion, but they urged him to go on.

He told them about the off-line meeting and about how the managers at Thiokol had been persuaded to change their minds. He also told them how he had continued to plead the case not to launch after the phone call was over.

When he was finished speaking, an exasperated Chairman Rogers looked at him. "Who the hell are you?" he asked.

"I'm the Director of the Solid Rocket Motor Project at Morton Thiokol."

"Would you please come down here and repeat what you've just said," Rogers said. "Because if I just heard what I think I heard, then this may be in litigation for years to come."

People from NASA, including Mulloy, had told them that Thiokol recommended to launch. Now they were hearing the opposite. Feynman and the commissioners didn't know what to believe.

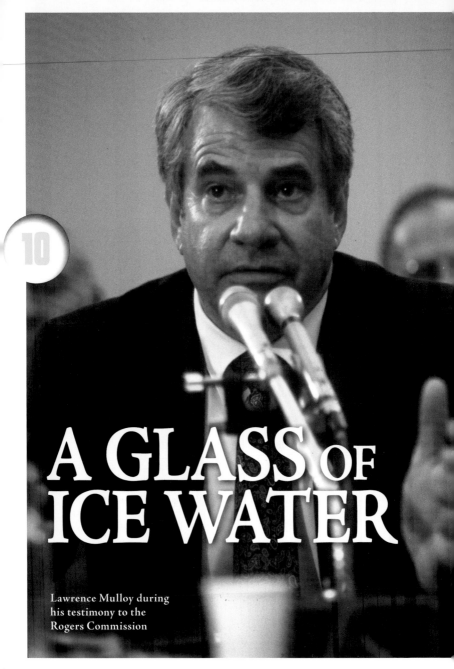

A GLASS OF
ICE WATER

Lawrence Mulloy during
his testimony to the
Rogers Commission

The commission meeting the next day
was public, and the press swarmed the
room. TV cameras filmed everything.

The crowd quieted as Lawrence Mulloy
was called again to speak. He continued to
assert that there was no reason to believe
that the O-rings would not perform well in
cold weather. They just did not have data
to prove it one way or the other.

Commissioner Feynman had said very
little so far. But the previous night he'd
come up with an idea. Once again he called
NASA chief Bill Graham. He asked if he
could get him an actual O-ring. At first
Graham thought this would be impossible,
but then he realized that there would be
a model circulating at the meeting
on Tuesday.

"All you need to do is take it out of the case when it's passed to you," he'd told Feynman.

Now Feynman sat with a C-clamp and a pair of pliers in his pockets. He intended to put pressure on the O-ring, submerge it in ice-cold water, and then take it out to see how it would react at a temperature of 32 degrees Fahrenheit. It seemed absurd that NASA kept saying they couldn't figure out whether cold would affect the O-rings when all they had to do was test it.

But Feynman had no ice water. Every day prior to this, the commissioners had been supplied with ice water. But today it had been overlooked. He pulled an attendant aside and asked for water.

On and on Mulloy spoke while Feynman waited. He fidgeted in his seat, eager to conduct his experiment. He decided to ask Mulloy a few questions of his own to set the stage. He asked about how the O-rings expand when the joints shift and vibrate, thus keeping the hot gasses inside the rocket.

Feynman said, "In the seal, in order to work correctly, the O-rings must be made of rubber—not something like lead."

"Yes, sir," Mulloy said.

"Now, if the O-rings weren't resilient for a second or two, would that be enough to be a very serious situation?"

"Yes, sir," Mulloy responded.

Finally the O-ring model was passed to Feynman, and he pulled the segment out of the model. A moment later, his water arrived. Feynman clamped the O-ring segment so that it was compressed, then dropped it into the glass of ice water. A few minutes passed during which Mulloy continued to answer questions from the commissioners. Feynman was waiting for just the right moment to reveal his experiment.

Finally Feynman said that he would like to make a comment. He said, "I took this stuff that I got out of your seals and I put it in ice water, and I discovered that when you put pressure on it for a while and then undo it, it doesn't stretch back. It stays the same dimension."

He unscrewed the C-clamp from the O-ring segment and held it up so the TV cameras and news photographers could get a good shot of it.

"In other words," he said, "for a few seconds at least—and more seconds than that—there is no resilience in this particular material when it is at a temperature of 32 degrees Fahrenheit.

I believe that has some significance for our problem."

Mulloy looked paralyzed. Feynman had just used a simple experiment, one that everyone around the country could see on TV and easily understand, to show exactly what had gone wrong with *Challenger*. After hours and hours of research and testimony—indeed, after years of the space shuttle project—Mulloy and others had been unable, or unwilling, to reach the same conclusion.

Richard Feynman showed reporters the O-ring he tested in a glass of ice water.

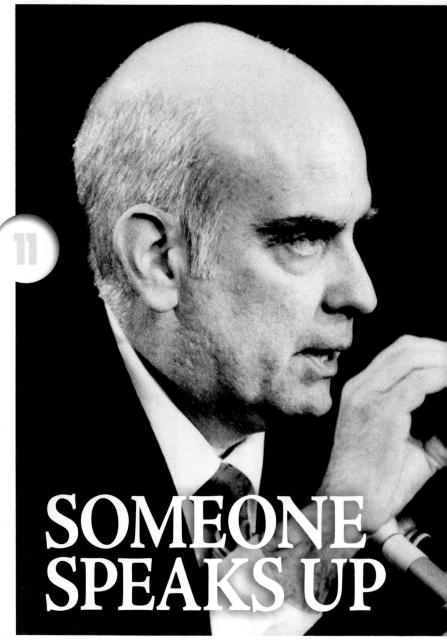

SOMEONE SPEAKS UP

Roger Boisjoly speaking to the Rogers Commission

Roger Boisjoly

Because of Allan McDonald's revealing testimony two days earlier, several Morton Thiokol employees and NASA employees were being called to testify before the Rogers Commission on Friday, February 14. To prepare for this meeting, Thiokol management had a meeting the night before with everyone who was going to appear.

Among the Thiokol employees in the crowded meeting room was Roger Boisjoly, who had felt sick with guilt ever since the disaster. Though he had opposed the launch and spoke up about it fervently, he believed he could have done more to prevent it. He could have called someone higher up at NASA to explain the risk. Or he could have called the president of the United States! Instead he sat by as his bosses approved the launch.

Now Thiokol had a team of lawyers at the front of the room. "When commissioners ask you a question, you should respond only with a yes or no," one of the lawyers told them. "You do not need to volunteer any information that is not specifically asked for, and you should not do so. Tell the truth, but don't give any more information than you have to."

Boisjoly realized that Thiokol planned to do what NASA had done—stonewall the commission to avoid blame and embarrassment. His ill feeling grew even stronger.

Just then McDonald stood up. He told the lawyers and everyone else that the commission was too important. They were trying to find out the truth of what happened so that it could be avoided in the future. If Thiokol employees were not honest about what happened, the facts might never come out.

"It's my intent tomorrow," McDonald said, "to tell the commission everything I know about the circumstances leading up to the accident in as much detail as I can remember."

At first, the room was silent. Then Boisjoly spoke up. "I agree with Al, and I'm going to do the same thing."

The room erupted in arguments and complaints. Managers glared at McDonald and Boisjoly. Boisjoly knew that speaking honestly at the commission would hurt his bosses and friends he worked with. It could cost his company millions of dollars in future contracts, and it could get him fired. But he knew what he had to do.

Roger Boisjoly and Allan McDonald

All the Morton Thiokol employees were sworn in by the commission. They could be punished by law if they didn't tell the truth.

While Thiokol managers Jerry Mason and Bob Lund were answering questions about the decision to launch, someone in the audience stood up to make a comment. His name was Bob Crippen, and he was a former astronaut.

He said, "Since the earliest days of the manned space flight program, our basic philosophy is: Prove to me we're ready to fly. And somehow it seems, in this particular instance, we have switched around to: Prove to me we are not able to fly. I think that was a serious mistake on NASA's part, if that was the case."

This was what Roger Boisjoly thought too, and he was relieved to hear an astronaut make this statement. Of all the people who worked on the shuttles, nobody put their lives at stake the way the astronauts did. Crippen's words carried weight.

Then Richard Feynman asked Mason and Lund, "Could you tell me the names of your four best seal experts, in order of their ability?"

Lund responded, "Roger Boisjoly, Arnie Thompson, Jack Kapp, and Jerry Burns."

"What was the opinion of your top two experts?" Feynman asked. "Did they agree that it was OK to fly?"

At this Boisjoly spoke up. "No, sir, we did not agree. And we never changed our minds."

Commissioner Rogers asked how many engineers were on the seal team, and Thompson told him there were 24 or 25.

Rogers asked, "All of those people would have said no to the launch?"

Thompson said, "My judgment is yes, that is true."

Finally it was Boisjoly's turn to tell his side of the story. He explained that he had been warning management about the reliability of the O-rings for months. He described the O-rings as turning into bricks when it was cold. He produced the memo he'd written the previous summer spelling out the dangers quite clearly—a memo that had gone ignored. He showed the same photos and charts that he'd shown everyone at the prelaunch meeting on January 27. And then he described what happened in Utah when the Thiokol team members went off-line for their private discussion.

"Our people asked for a five-minute caucus to discuss the situation," Boisjoly said. "Myself and Mr. Thompson continued to press our case with MTI management, opposing the launch. And we did everything we could to continue to try and press for not launching. I took the photographic position of the evidence and Mr. Thompson was trying to further elaborate on the characteristics of the seals.

"When we realized that we basically had stopped in the discussion and we could go no further because we were getting nowhere, we backed off, both of us. We just sat back down."

Then one of the commissioners asked, "What was the motivation driving those trying to overturn your opposition?"

"They felt that I had not conclusively demonstrated that there was a tie-in between temperature and blowby. I felt personally that management was under a lot of pressure to launch."

Later in the questioning, Jerry Mason explained that they didn't have any solid rules for when it was OK to launch. There was no regulation that said don't launch below 53 degrees—they were only guessing. Every time a shuttle flew, it was adding new data. "So every flight in this program has had to break some frontiers," he said.

Sally Ride got quite upset at this comment. "The time you go through frontiers is during testing, not during the flights. That's the way it's supposed to work!"

Later when the commission was about to finish for the day, Allan McDonald stood up again. "I would like to testify," he said.

McDonald then described the meeting from his side, including his pleading with Lawrence Mulloy while they waited for Joe Kilminster's signed launch approval to arrive by fax. McDonald had described three reasons not to launch. First the O-ring engineers believed that the O-rings were not resilient in the cold. Second the ice on the pad could cause damage to the craft. And third the weather in the ocean where the recovery ships were supposed to pick up the SRBs was highly dangerous at that time.

At the end of his testimony, one of the commissioners asked him if he felt he was put under intense pressure by NASA to launch, in spite of the warnings.

"Yes," McDonald said. "That is true."

Allan McDonald being sworn in before
the Rogers Commission

McDonald and Boisjoly felt the eyes of their bosses and colleagues from Thiokol burning into them. They had just made it clear to the whole world that Morton Thiokol and NASA had decided to risk the lives of seven astronauts even though they knew it wasn't safe.

As they left the room, McDonald couldn't help tearing up. He and Boisjoly were both exhausted and devastated. Though they'd done what they believed to be the right thing, it felt painful.

But at that moment, something happened that made them feel better. Sally Ride approached them and thanked them. "I'm glad someone finally leveled with this commission," she said, and gave them both hugs. Here was a real hero, someone who had risked her own life to go into space. She had put her safety into the hands of people at NASA and Thiokol. It was people like her that McDonald and Boisjoly were fighting for.

Members of the commission, including William Rogers
(left) and Sally Ride (right), examined pieces of the
shuttle to find out what caused it to explode.

RECOVERY

Wreckage from the space shuttle, including this piece of the crew compartment, were put on large Navy ships and brought to shore.

Mike McAllister was almost out of breathing air. He and his diving partner, Terry Bailey, were 87 feet below the surface of the ocean and about to head back up when they saw a silvery shape moving in the darkness.

Visibility this far below the surface was very low, especially because bad weather had stirred up silt. They could see only about an arm's length in front of them. But McAllister thought they'd better get a closer look at that ... what was it?

It looked like a pair of legs.

McAllister's heart began to pound hard. He didn't expect to find any dead bodies down here! He wasn't sure he was ready to face such a sight. He'd been searching the ocean for six weeks now, and he hadn't found anything like that.

Moving closer, though, he realized it was the bottom half of a spacesuit pinned under something and waving in the current. The legs had filled with air and floated toward the surface. He breathed a sigh of relief that it wasn't a body.

But then he tensed again as he remembered that the spacesuits were stored in the crew cabin. That meant the cabin was nearby. He and Bailey moved forward toward the spacesuit. As they did the crumpled metal frame of the crew cabin emerged from the dark and murky water in front of them. The crew lay inside those mangled metal posts.

In part of his mind, McAllister thought, "Jackpot! This is what we've been looking for!"

But another part of his mind was saddened and disturbed. It was a grim and eerie scene.

The two divers had little time to contemplate the moment, however. They needed to get up to fresh air. So they marked the spot with a buoy and ascended to their ship.

Over the next two days, the cabin and bodies were pulled from the ocean. By now everyone knew what had caused the explosion. They had watched the video footage many times, and they had seen the photos of the black puffs of gas leaking from the SRBs. The press had reported on the interviews in the Rogers Commission, and they knew about the disturbing decision to launch. But many people had still felt unsettled about the *Challenger* disaster, knowing that the bodies were still lost. Now that the crew had been recovered, it finally felt like the horrible event was drawing to a close.

There was only one big question remaining. Would a space shuttle ever fly again?

Allan McDonald

The weather was warm this time.

After two and a half years of work, NASA was ready to launch another space shuttle. *Discovery* stood on the launchpad. When the SRBs boomed to life and white clouds of exhaust expanded below them, *Discovery* lifted off the ground. It climbed steadily into the air, higher and higher, without incident.

From the launch control center, Allan McDonald watched it soar through the sky on a video screen. He had played a key role in the redesign of the SRBs. They had undergone severe scrutiny every step of the way. This time he knew they would perform as they were supposed to. Still, as he watched *Discovery* fly, he couldn't help but feel relief. He let out a long breath.

The September 29, 1988, launch of *Discovery* marked the United States' return to manned space flight.

It was never certain that he would be a part of the redesign. After their damaging testimony to the Rogers Commission, both he and Roger Boisjoly were reassigned to lesser jobs at Thiokol. Friends and peers at the company isolated and shunned them. But when U.S. Congressman Edward Markey learned of this treatment, he wrote a letter to the CEO of Morton Thiokol. He said that Thiokol would be barred from any future contracts with NASA if McDonald and Boisjoly were not reinstated to their original jobs and made a part of the redesign team.

McDonald embraced the second chance. He worked long and hard on the redesign, and he made sure everything was done right.

But Boisjoly had a harder time. His July memo about the dangers of the O-rings was considered a bombshell. It broke open the investigation and showed the world just how the risky decision was made.

Boisjoly took the rejection by his colleagues very hard, and after a while, he left the company. He grew deeply depressed. He had headaches and double vision. He became grumpy with his own family and generally tried to avoid people.

It was a heavy price to pay for being right.

This launch, though, was the culmination of many, many hours of hard work for McDonald and others. As he felt the SRBs' rumble deep in his stomach, McDonald swallowed a proud lump in his throat. The day *Challenger* exploded, President Reagan promised that America would continue to explore space. Those astronauts had lost their lives trying to expand our understanding of the universe, and we would honor them by continuing that expansion. The explosion was a setback, but it was not an end.

TIMELINE

July 19, 1985: Christa McAuliffe wins a national competition to be the first Teacher in Space.

July 1985: Roger Boisjoly reports in a Morton Thiokol memo that more people need to be assigned to fixing the O-ring problems. Then Richard Cook, resource analyst for NASA, writes a memo stating that the O-rings are not reliable and that a new joint needs to be designed.

January 27, 1986: All seven *Challenger* astronauts are stuck in the shuttle for five hours waiting for NASA technicians to fix a broken hatch handle. Finally the launch is scrubbed and rescheduled for the next day.

January 27, about 8:45 p.m.: Leaders from NASA and Morton Thiokol meet on a three-way conference call to decide if *Challenger* should launch the next day.

January 27, about 11:00 p.m.: Morton Thiokol agrees to recommend launching *Challenger* the next day.

January 28, 3:00 a.m.: NASA on-air commentator Hugh Harris arrives at the launch site. NASA crew members break up icicles hanging from the launch platform.

January 28, 8:00 a.m.: The astronauts enter the White Room, the area at the top of the launch platform tower where they prepare to board the shuttle.

January 28, 8:36 a.m.: The entire crew is on board *Challenger*, and the shuttle's hatch is closed.

January 28, 11:38 a.m.: *Challenger* has liftoff.

January 28, 11:39 a.m.: Seventy-three seconds after liftoff, the shuttle ignites into a ball of fire. The fire engulfs the shuttle.

January 28, 11:42 a.m.: At the Kennedy Space Center, the doors to the Launch Control Center are locked. The investigation into the explosion begins.

January 28, 11:42 a.m.: The shuttle hits the surface of the Atlantic Ocean at a speed greater than 200 miles per hour, crushing the cabin and killing everyone inside.

January 28, 4:40 p.m.: NASA holds a press conference to announce the tragedy.

January 28, 5:00 p.m.: President Ronald Reagan addresses the nation.

February 4: President Reagan creates the Rogers Commission to investigate the explosion.

February 9: *The New York Times* runs a front-page story quoting NASA memos proving that leaders were aware of the faulty O-rings.

February 10: The Rogers Commission holds a closed-door session to interview NASA employees.

February 11: The Rogers Commission holds a public meeting where Commissioner Feynman demonstrates how the O-rings failed.

February 13: Morton Thiokol holds a private meeting with employees who would be testifying before the Rogers Commission the next day. Allan McDonald and Roger Boisjoly announce that they will defy the company's orders to give as little information to the commission as possible.

February 14: McDonald and Boisjoly testify before the Rogers Commission. They confirm that they recommended not to launch. They also say that both NASA and Morton Thiokol executives made the decision to launch even though they knew it wasn't safe.

March 7: Diver Mike McAllister and his partner discover the remains of the crew at the bottom of the ocean.

September 29, 1988: NASA launches *Discovery*, the first space shuttle to take off since the *Challenger* disaster.

GLOSSARY

auxiliary power unit (awg-ZIL-ur-ee POW-ur-YOO-nit)—a device that provides the energy to run the electrical systems on large vehicles such as planes and spacecraft

console (KAHN-sole)—the control unit on a space shuttle or other large vehicle or computerized device

hydraulic power (hye-DRAW-lik POW-ur)—power made by circulating pressurized fluid; hydraulic power systems can be stronger than other types of power systems and are often used on spacecraft

mobile launch platform (MOW-buhl LAWNCH PLAT-fohrm)—a two-story movable building used by NASA at the Kennedy Space Center to support space shuttles during assembly, transportation to the launchpad, and as the shuttle's launch platform

orbiter (OR-bit-ur)—the main part of a space shuttle; the orbiter is the part of the shuttle that goes into space and returns to Earth

solid rocket booster (SAH-lid ROK-it BOO-stur)—a motor used to provide immediate power when a spaceship first launches from its launchpad

turbulence (TUR-byoo-luns)—swirling winds that create strong air resistance; turbulence can quickly slow down an aircraft

wind shear (WIND SHIHR)—a difference in wind speed and direction over a relatively short distance in the atmosphere

CRITICAL THINKING USING THE COMMON CORE

1. Why did the managers at Morton Thiokol change their minds about approving the launch? Compare their reasons for launching to NASA's reasons. (Key Ideas and Details)

2. Compare Richard Feynman's actions on pages 82–83 with Sally Ride's actions on pages 93 and 96. How did these commissioners' personal experiences influence their actions and perspectives on the disaster? (Craft and Structure)

3. When Allan McDonald and Roger Boisjoly testified in front of the commission, they disobeyed their bosses' instructions to say as little as possible, putting their careers at risk. What else were they risking? Why did they do it? Using other texts, compare their actions to the actions of other whistle-blowers in history. (Integration of Knowledge and Ideas)

INTERNET SITES

FactHound offers a safe, fun way to find Internet sites related to this book. All of the sites on FactHound have been researched by our staff.

Here's all you do:
Visit www.facthound.com
Type in this code: 9781491470770

FactHound will fetch the best sites for you!

FURTHER READING

Burgess, Colin. *Teacher in Space: Christa McAuliffe and the Challenger Legacy.* Amazon Digital Services, Inc., 2014.

Holden, Henry M. *Space Shuttle Disaster: The Tragic Mission of the Challenger.* Berkeley Heights, N.J.: Enslow Publishers, 2013.

SELECTED BIBLIOGRAPHY

Barbree, Jay. "The Challenger Saga: An American Space Tragedy," NBCNews.com, originally published in January 1997.

Boffey, Philip M. "Analyst Who Gave Shuttle Warning Faults 'Gung-Ho, Can-Do' Attitude," *New York Times*, February 14, 1986.

Boffey, Philip M. "Challenger Crew Knew of Problem, Data Now Suggest," *New York Times*, July 29, 1986.

Boisjoly, Roger M. "SRM O-Ring Erosion/Potential Failure Criticality," internal Morton Thiokol memo originally published July 31, 1985. Reprinted in Letters of Note, http://www.lettersofnote.com/2009/10/result-would-be-catastrophe.html

Boisjoly, Roger M. "The Challenger Disaster: Moral Responsibility and the Working Engineer," *Ethical Issues in Engineering*, Deborah Johnson, ed. Prentice Hall, Englewood Cliffs, N.J., 1991.

Broad, William J. "The Shuttle Explodes," *New York Times*, January 29, 1986.

Cook, Richard C. *Challenger Revealed: An Insider's Account of How the Reagan Administration Caused the Greatest Tragedy of the Space Age.* New York: Thunder's Mouth Press, 2006.

Corrigan, Grace. *A Journal for Christa.* Lincoln, Neb.: University of Nebraska Press, 1993.

"Divers Saw Flight Suit in Shuttle Wreck," *New York Times*, July 15, 1986.

Harris, Hugh. *Challenger: An American Tragedy.* New York: Open Road Integrated Media, 2014.

Herron, Caroline Rand, and Martha A. Miles. "After Challenger, Hope and Trouble," *New York Times*, February 1, 1987.

Jensen, Claus. *No Downlink: A Dramatic Narrative About the Challenger Accident and Our Time.* New York: Farrar, Straus, Giroux, 1993. Translated from Danish by Barbara Haveland in 1996.

McDonald, Allan J., with James R. Hansen. *Truth, Lies, and O-Rings: Inside the Space Shuttle Challenger Disaster.* Gainesville, Fla.: University of Florida Press, 2009.

Reagan, Ronald. "Explosion of the Space Shuttle Challenger: Address to the Nation, January 28, 1986." History.nasa.gov/reagan12886.html

Rodgers, June Scobee. *Silver Linings: Triumph of the Challenger 7.* Macon, Ga.: Peake Road, 1996.

Sanger, David E. "A Year Later, Two Engineers Cope with Challenger Horror," *New York Times*, January 28, 1987.

Sanger, David E. "Engineers Tell of Punishment for Shuttle Testimony," *New York Times*, May 11, 1986.

Schmidt, William E. "All Shuttle Crew Remains Recovered, NASA Says," *New York Times*, April 20, 1986.

Vaughan, Diane. *The Challenger Launch Decision.* Chicago: University of Chicago Press, 1996.

INDEX

ABOUT THE AUTHOR

Eric Braun has written dozens of books for readers of all ages, and he has always been fascinated by outer space. His picture book *If I Were an Astronaut* was awarded the Eugene M. Emme Astronautical Literature Award, and he was recently awarded a McKnight Artist Fellowship in writing. He lives in Minneapolis with his wife, two sons, a dog, and a gecko.